SAVING OUR WORLD

RAINFORESTS

Jane Parker

COPPER BEECH BOOKS
BROOKFIELD, CONNECTICUT

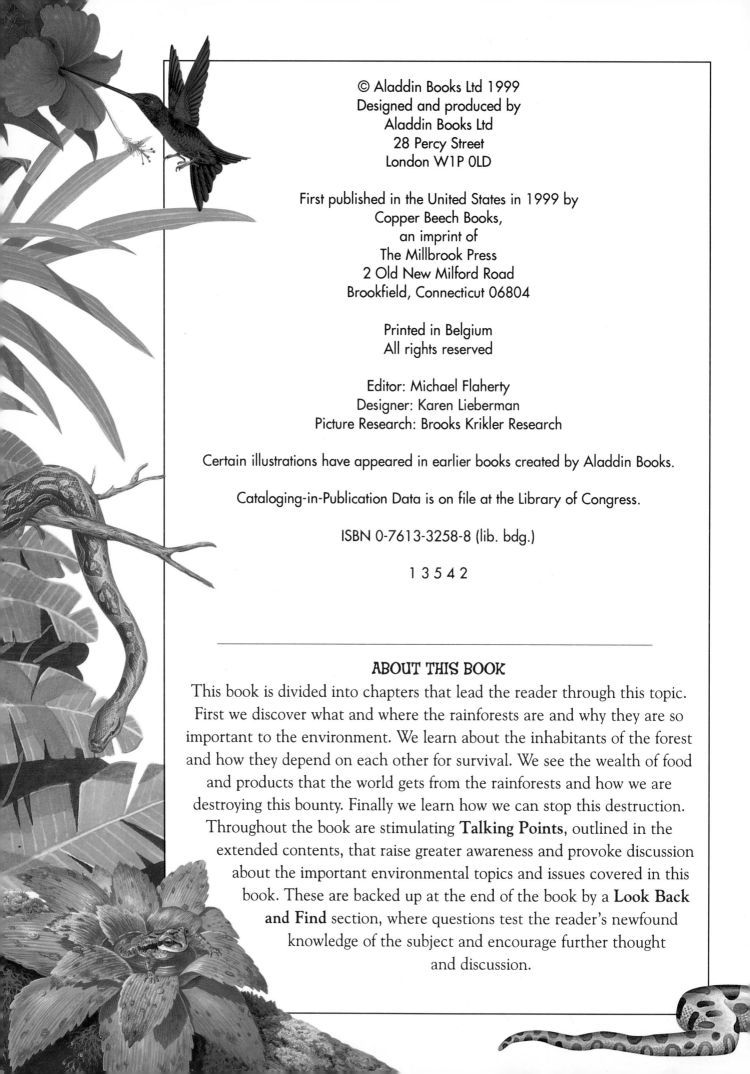

© Aladdin Books Ltd 1999
Designed and produced by
Aladdin Books Ltd
28 Percy Street
London W1P 0LD

First published in the United States in 1999 by
Copper Beech Books,
an imprint of
The Millbrook Press
2 Old New Milford Road
Brookfield, Connecticut 06804

Editor: Michael Flaherty
Designer: Karen Lieberman
Picture Research: Brooks Krikler Research

Certain illustrations have appeared in earlier books created by Aladdin Books.

Cataloging-in-Publication Data is on file at the Library of Congress.

ISBN 0-7613-3258-8 (lib. bdg.)

1 3 5 4 2

ABOUT THIS BOOK

This book is divided into chapters that lead the reader through this topic.
First we discover what and where the rainforests are and why they are so
important to the environment. We learn about the inhabitants of the forest
and how they depend on each other for survival. We see the wealth of food
and products that the world gets from the rainforests and how we are
destroying this bounty. Finally we learn how we can stop this destruction.
Throughout the book are stimulating **Talking Points**, outlined in the
extended contents, that raise greater awareness and provoke discussion
about the important environmental topics and issues covered in this
book. These are backed up at the end of the book by a **Look Back
and Find** section, where questions test the reader's newfound
knowledge of the subject and encourage further thought
and discussion.

Contents

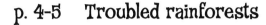

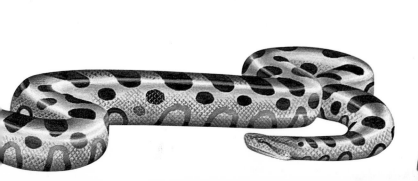

Troubled Rainforests

The green, lush rainforest

Most mornings in a tropical rainforest the sunshine beats down on the trees, and then in the afternoon thunderous storms drench every leaf and flower. This warmth and dampness is just right for plants to grow. And where there are plants there are animals to eat

In fact, more plants and animals live in rainforests than anywhere else on earth Rainforests are also home to many groups of people. But we all need the rainforests. The trees help to keep the earth's air fresh for us to breathe and they also have an important part in shaping the world's weather cycle.

Many trees crowd together to reach up to the light.

Thick growth showing a healthy rainforest.

Dead forest due to cutting and burning trees.

The dying rainforests

The rainforests are precious. Yet people are destroying them, chopping down the trees, burning the plants, and killing the animals. They do this to make money by selling the wood and farming the land. Some say that if the destruction does not stop, all the rainforests, and their plants and animals, will be gone by the year 2050.

Once gone, the forests will never grow back as they were. The nutrients in the soil will be used up, and the rain will wash the thin soil away. The plants and animals will have died, and forest people will have lost their way of life.

CHAPTER ONE

What is a Rainforest?

Rainforests of the World

Tropical rainforests grow in a wide band around the middle of the earth, stretching across an area above and below the Equator, between two imaginary lines called the Tropics. It is always warm here, about 77°F (25°C), and more than 78 in. (200 cm) of rain fall every year.

Around the world

Tropical rainforests once grew across all tropical lands. Now there are only patches left in Central and South America, central Africa, India, Southeast Asia, and northeastern Australia. The map (right) shows the areas where forest still exists and where it has been destroyed.

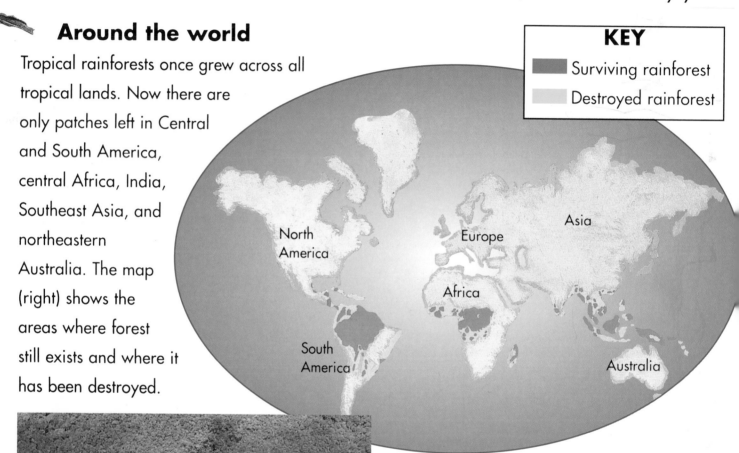

KEY
Surviving rainforest
Destroyed rainforest

North America

Europe

Asia

Africa

South America

Australia

The Amazon rainforest

The biggest rainforest is in South America (left). It covers 2.5 million sq. miles (6 million sq. km.). It is so vast that a person could walk for over 2,000 miles (3,200 kilometers) without seeing the sky between the treetops. Streams and rivers, flowing between the tree trunks, meet up to become the largest river in the world — the Amazon River.

◀ Mangrove forest

Mangrove trees grow where the rainforest meets the sea. They live with their roots in salty mud that would kill most plants. They have special "breathing" roots that poke up above the mud in a tangle of stilts and knobbly arches.

◀ Lowland forest

Lowland rainforests stretch between the mountains and the coast. The trees are called broad-leaved evergreens because they don't lose their broad, flat leaves all at the same time of year.

Temperate forest ▶

Temperate rainforests grow just outside the Tropics, where it is cooler and wet in the winter and warm and drier in the summer. Very tall conifers, like redwoods, grow in the temperate rainforests of North America, and gum trees grow in Australia.

▲ Montane and cloud forest

Where the forest climbs up the cooler mountain slopes, it becomes shrouded in the soaking fog of the clouds. The leaves drip constantly and every trunk and twig is draped in thick, spongy moss.

TALKING POINT

Q: Does it rain every day of the year in the rainforests? How much rain falls in a year?

A: It rains almost every day in the rainforest. About 2,900 cubic miles of rain fall every year on the Amazon rainforest — that's the amount of water in Lake Superior, the largest of the North American Great Lakes!

Multistory Rainforest

There is a constant battle going on inside a rainforest as every plant struggles to reach the sunlight. The trees grow as tall as they can and spread their leafy branches to the sky. Beneath, the plants and animals live in layers of increasing darkness down toward the dim forest floor.

Layers in the rainforest

The leafy tree branches form a roof, or canopy, that shuts out most of the sunlight. Here and there an extra-tall tree, called an emergent, towers above the canopy. Below is the understory; it is a tangle of creepers, vines, air plants, and the fronds of palms and tree ferns. Little grows on the forest floor except fungi and young sapling trees awaiting a gap in the canopy above.

The tallest trees are called emergents.

Canopy layer — most of the animals live here.

Forest recyclers live on the forest floor.

Understory — the forest highway

Shrubs and ferns grow in the darkness.

Buttress supports

The forest soil is very thin, so the huge trees grow great triangular supports, or buttresses, out of the sides of their trunks to prop them up. The trees also support each other because their branches are bound together by the thick, twining stems of creepers and vines.

Dripping leaves

Most of the forest leaves have smooth, waxy surfaces with long, pointed drip-tips (above). They are held at an angle on their stems so the rain runs right off. This keeps water from collecting in pools that would rot the leaves or allow a layer of tiny plants to grow and block out the light.

Strangler fig

A strangler fig begins its life high on the branch of a forest tree. It sends down roots that gradually surround the trunk and strangle the tree to death. The dead tree rots away, leaving the fig (right) surrounding a hollow space.

TALKING POINT Rainforest trees are among the world's tallest trees. Some emergent trees are 270 ft. (80 m) tall — almost as tall as the Statue of Liberty!

Q: Do they have deep roots to support them, like the deep taproots of trees like oak trees, or do they have shallow roots?

A: They have very shallow roots that spread far and wide beneath the leaf litter to find water and nutrients

The Earth's Green Lungs

Tropical rainforests are sometimes called the lungs of the world. This is because the trees give out oxygen, a gas that all living things need to breathe. Oxygen is just one of the chemicals, along with water and carbon, that pass through the forests in great, never-ending cycles.

Water cycle

Water evaporates, or turns into a gas called water vapor, from rivers, lakes, and oceans. This gas rises up into the air, cools, and condenses, turning into water droplets in the clouds. The droplets fall back to the ground as rain. Some of this water sinks into the ground, and some of it washes across the land back into rivers, lakes, and oceans.

Water evaporates from the plants.

Sun

Rain falls from clouds.

Plants absorb the water.

All animals, like this tree frog, need the water to live.

Thin soil layer

Groundwater

River

Water evaporates from the water surface by sun's heat.

River runs to the sea.

Flooding

Forests are sometimes deliberately flooded. When this happens the plants die and begin to rot away. As they rot the carbon locked in their stems, leaves and roots is released as carbon dioxide gas into the air. The rotting process uses up the oxygen in the water and turns it into a smelly stagnant soup.

Burning forests

When the forests burn, the billowing clouds of smoke contain ash, soot, and gases such as carbon dioxide. This is one of a group of gases called "greenhouse gases," which help to keep the sun's heat in the earth's atmosphere. Too much of these gases may trap too much of the sun's heat.

Carbon cycle

Plants take in carbon from the air as carbon dioxide gas. They combine it with water to turn it into food and plant tissue by using the sun's energy. This releases oxygen into the air, which plants and animals need to breathe. Animals eat plants and breathe carbon dioxide back out into the air. When the trees are cleared there are less plants to take up the carbon dioxide and release oxygen.

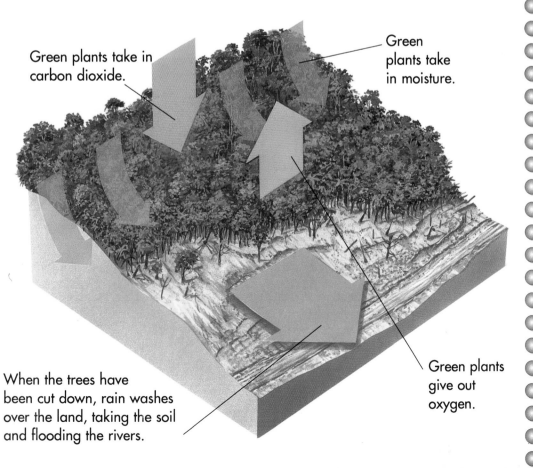

Green plants take in carbon dioxide.

Green plants take in moisture.

Green plants give out oxygen.

When the trees have been cut down, rain washes over the land, taking the soil and flooding the rivers.

TALKING POINT

Carbon dioxide is one of the gases that help to keep the earth warm. When this gas builds up in the air, the earth's temperature may rise. This is called global warming.

Q: What are the effects of global warming?

A: As global warming increases, scientists predict such catastrophes as the melting of the polar ice caps. This would cause a rise in sea level, leading to increased coastal erosion and flooding of lowland forests, cities, and farmland. There would also be dramatic changes in weather patterns.

11

CHAPTER TWO

Life in the Rainforest

How the Rainforest Works

Every plant and animal in the forest depends upon the plants and animals that live around it. They need each other for food, for shelter, and sometimes for support. These close relationships make up an ecosystem.

Food chains of the forest

Energy comes into the forest as sunlight and is turned into food by green plants. Plant-eating animals are called herbivores. Animals called carnivores eat other animals.

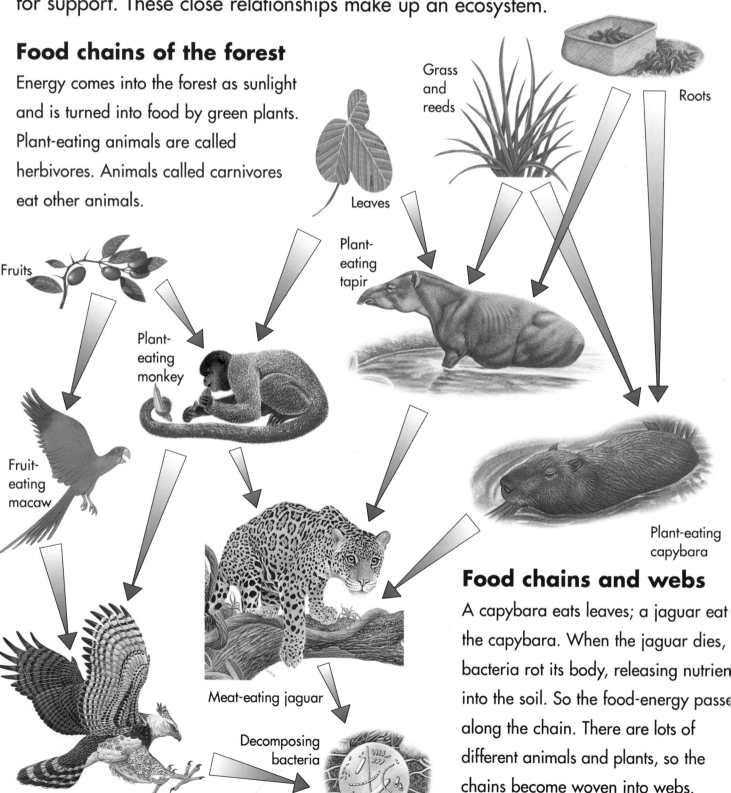

Grass and reeds

Roots

Leaves

Fruits

Plant-eating tapir

Plant-eating monkey

Fruit-eating macaw

Plant-eating capybara

Meat-eating jaguar

Decomposing bacteria

Meat-eating harpy eagle

Food chains and webs

A capybara eats leaves; a jaguar eat the capybara. When the jaguar dies, bacteria rot its body, releasing nutrien into the soil. So the food-energy passe along the chain. There are lots of different animals and plants, so the chains become woven into webs.

Sun

Sunlight is absorbed by the green coloring, or pigment, in leaves.

Effects of sunlight

Plants trap the energy in sunlight by a special chemical process called photosynthesis. The green colored substance in their leaves absorbs the light so the energy can be used to make sugary food. The plants then use the food to grow.

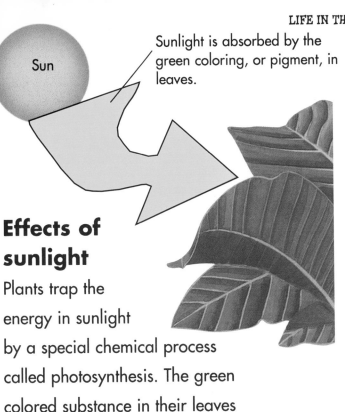

No waste

Nothing is ever wasted in the forest; everything is eaten by something else. Dead things and droppings are devoured on the ground by an army of decomposers, including insects and other small animals, fungi, and tiny bacteria.

Fungi growing on dead leaves and logs

Bacteria break down anything that remains.

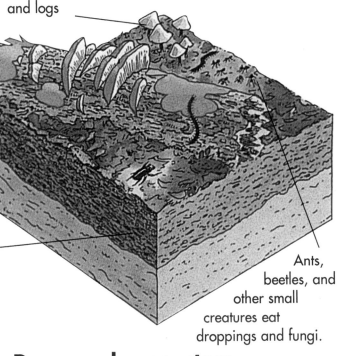

Ants, beetles, and other small creatures eat droppings and fungi.

Damaged ecosystem

The ecosystem in an undisturbed rainforest is delicately balanced and easily upset. If, for example, the trees are cut or burned, the monkeys have no food and die. Then the eagles have no food or place to raise their chicks, and they die. Even if the trees grow back, the animals may not be replaced.

TALKING POINT Everything in the forest is eaten by something else. Look back at the food web on the last page.

Q: Can you name some forest foods and who might eat them? Try to figure out the food chains of some animals you know.

A: Here is an example: butterflies drink flower nectar; birds eat butterflies; cats eat birds; bacteria and fungi rot dead cats.

13

Rainforest Partnerships

Many plants and animals in the forest form partnerships to help them survive. Often these partnerships are so close that one partner cannot live without the other. Not all partnerships benefit both partners. Some are based on trickery and deception, such as the pitcher plant's (see page 15).

Harpy eagle

Golden-headed parakeet

Sloth

Allen's opossum

Tree snake

Howler monkeys

Macaw

Squirrel monkey

Morpho butterfly

Canopy creatures

About half of all the world's animals probably live in the rainforests, but no one really knows for sure because new kinds, especially insects, are being discovered all the time. Most of these creatures live high in the canopy where there is food, and places to hide are plentiful. The tree branches form a highway for some animals to scamper or slither across. It is a place for birds to build their nests and also a place for many smaller plants to grow so they can reach the sunlight.

Animal–eaters

Some plants, like the pitcher plants (left), get extra nourishment by being carnivorous. They lure insect victims with the perfume of sweet nectar, but there is no nectar, just a deadly tank of digestive juices and rainwater, with a very slippery rim!

Hummingbird

Pollination

Flowers bribe animals with nectar to carry their pollen to other flowers, to fertilize the seeds. Hummingbirds delve into the flowers, get covered in powdery pollen, and fly off to the next flower.

Sowing seeds

Some plants wrap their seeds in appetising fruit. Animals swallow both fruit and seeds, then drop the seeds around the forest.

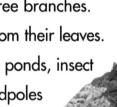

Mini-ecosystem

Bromeliad plants (right) live high up on tree branches. They collect water in little ponds formed from their leaves. Tiny water plants called algae grow in the ponds, insect larvae feed on the algae, and tree frog tadpoles feed on the larvae. There is even a little crab that sometimes lives here.

Frog in a bromeliad pond

Many forest plants depend upon animals to spread their seeds.

Q: What would happen if the animals disappeared?

A: The seeds would not be spread around the forest, but would fall into the darkness around the parent tree. The seeds would sprout, but the young plants would have to wait until their parent died and fell before there would be any light for them to grow.

Rainforest People

Small groups of people have lived in rainforests for thousands of years, isolated from each other by miles of jungle. They have learned to survive by taking everything they need — but nothing more — from the forest. They live in harmony with and do little damage to the forest. But now their home is disappearing fast.

Harvesting sweet potatoes from a forest clearing

Food from the forest

Forest people know which plants and animals — even grubs and spiders — are good to eat, and which ones are poisonous. They know when each tree is likely to fruit, how to catch the animals, and how to prepare the food so that it tastes good.

Slash and burn

Rainforest people usually live in small groups. When they need to grow crops, they cut down and burn a small area of trees and plant crops. After two or three years they move to another area. The damaged forest gradually heals its wound. On a bigger scale this type of farming does a lot of damage to the forest.

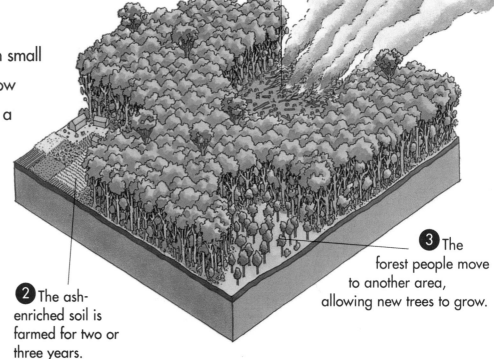

1 A small section of the forest is cut and burned.

2 The ash-enriched soil is farmed for two or three years.

3 The forest people move to another area, allowing new trees to grow.

Living in the forest

The people who live in the forest build strong houses to protect them from the heavy rain and the large animals. They use wood, bark, bamboo poles, leaves, and creeper stems. When they move on, the houses will be eaten by forest decomposers.

Year	Number of native people in the Brazilian rainforest
1992	200,000
1500	6-9 Million

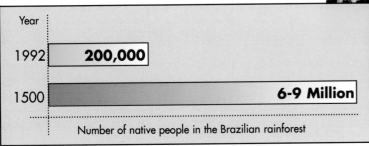

An Amazon hunter with a poison-tipped arrow (below)

Declining populations

Since Christopher Columbus first discovered South America in 1498, the number of Amerindians living in the Amazon rainforest has fallen by almost 98%. This is due to many factors, including European diseases like influenza.

Hunting in the rainforest

Animals are difficult to find in the forest. Large ones are rare and they are very secretive. Most animals live high in the treetops where they are very difficult to catch. Forest people use darts tipped with poison from brightly colored poisonous frogs (right).

TALKING POINT

There are fewer tribal people living in all the rainforests today.

Q: What do you think the reasons for this are?

A: At first they died from new diseases and infections, such as the common cold and influenza, brought in by European explorers. Many were slaughtered or put into slavery. Now some have to move deeper into the forest to hunt away from the destruction. Others are lured away by modern life.

CHAPTER THREE

Rainforest Bounty

Fruits of the Forest

The forest provides a bountiful harvest of fruits and other products. Perhaps the most obvious is wood. The wood of slow-growing rainforest trees is hard and strong. The trunks are tall and straight, with few branch scars (called knots). Some is used to make beautiful furniture, and some is pulped to make paper.

Daily supplies

The list of everyday rainforest products includes bamboo poles and canes, rattan woven into mats, spices such as nutmeg and ginger, coffee and cocoa (chocolate) beans and tea leaves, oils used for cooking, face creams, or machinery, and many others.

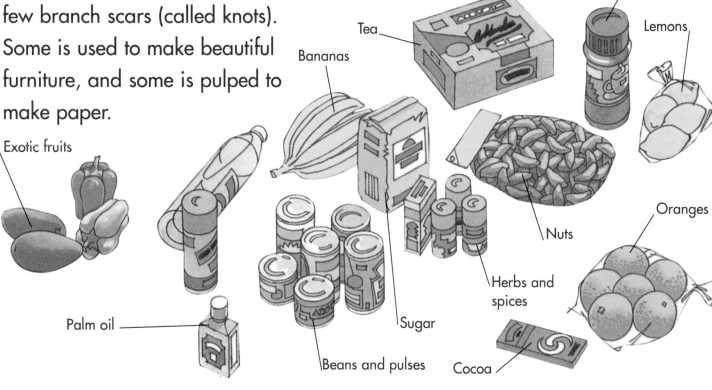

Exotic fruits

Palm oil

Bananas

Tea

Coffee

Lemons

Nuts

Oranges

Herbs and spices

Sugar

Beans and pulses

Cocoa

Selling the fruits

Many rainforest fruits, such as bananas – now grown on huge plantations where the forests used to be – are familiar all over the world. But local farmers (left) still grow plants, like sweet potatoes, on a smaller scale and take them to local markets.

Different woods

Melanti

Brazilian mahogany

Sapele

Timber from rainforest trees, like teak and mahogany, is called hardwood. It is difficult to cut but very strong and has a fine, straight grain. Timber from cooler pine forests is called softwood. It is easier to cut but it has less strength, and its grain is often marked with knots.

Mahogony

Mahogony is a beautiful wood that has been used for hundreds of years to make fine furniture (left). Sadly, it is now extremely rare in the wild due to over-logging.

House plants

Today many people bring the jungle into their homes by buying plants such as the Christmas cactus (right) and the shiny-leaved Swiss cheese plant.

Rubber tapping

Rubber is made from a gum called latex that oozes from wounds in the bark of certain trees (left). The latex sets and heals the wound.

People called rubber tappers make new cuts in the bark every few days and collect the latex in little cups (left). Latex is called a renewable harvest because gathering it does no permanent damage.

TALKING POINT

One third of the wood taken from rainforests ends up as paper for newspapers, magazines, books, tissues, and packaging.

Q: How can this huge amount be reduced?

A: By recycling as much used paper as possible; by buying products made from recycled paper; by not buying heavily packaged products; and by using writing paper thoughtfully.

CHAPTER FOUR

Damaging the Forest

Rainforests in Peril

The rainforests of the world are being destroyed at the staggering rate of 100 acres (40 hectares) — that's 60 soccer fields — every single minute! And despite years of protests, the logging, burning, and pollution of the land shows no sign of stopping while there is still money to be made.

Road building ▲

The loggers build roads deep into the forest so that they can get their machines in and the logs out. Settlers follow the loggers and clear the virgin (unspoiled) forest on either side of the roads. They grow crops or graze animals to make a quick cash profit so they can feed their families.

Logging ▼

The trees are mostly felled by huge machines that strip off the branches at the same time. Then they are hauled out of the forest on massive trailers. The falling trees and the colossal wheels of the machines flatten all the other plants so that everything is destroyed.

Man cutting down trees

Area cleared due to logging

Ranching ▶

Ranchers own large areas of the Amazon forest. They clear and burn the jungle plants and grow grass to feed cows. The cows are eventually killed to make burgers for fast-food restaurants. But the nutrients in the soil run out after 3 or 4 years, so the ranchers have to clear even more forest.

◀ Building dams

Falling water can be used to make cheap electricity called hydroelectricity. So, in many places, rivers are dammed to make lakes that contain enough water to turn the generating machines. When these lakes flood part of a rainforest, the plants and most of the animals are drowned.

Mining in the forest ▶

There are mines in many parts of the world's rainforests, especially the Amazon, which produce iron, copper, manganese, aluminum, nickel, or gold. The mines destroy trees and cause pollution with poisonous chemicals like mercury.

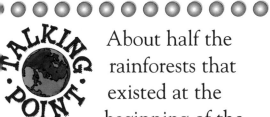

About half the rainforests that existed at the beginning of the 20th century were destroyed by the year 1999.

Q: How quickly are the rainforests being destroyed (see page 20)? How long will these forests last at this rate?

A: If the destruction continues, there may not be any rainforests left by 2050! That means the extinction of millions of animals and plants.

Endangered Animals

Endangered means threatened with extinction — extinction means gone forever! The forests are teeming with different kinds of animals, but there are often not many individuals of each kind. If their forest home is destroyed, they may not survive.

Gentle manatee

These peaceful animals feed on water weeds in the Amazon River. Some are hunted for meat, but many are killed accidentally by fishermen or by pollution.

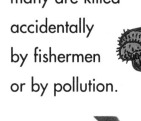

Man of the forest

This is what "orangutan" means in Sumatra where it lives. It is rare because the forest is being destroyed and because thousands of mother orangutans have been killed. Sometimes their babies are taken for the pet trade.

Manatee

Orangutan

Gorilla

Gorillas

The rarest gorillas are mountain gorillas (right) that live in the montane forests of Central Africa. Even though they are protected by law, these huge animals are killed by poachers who sell their heads, hands, and feet as "ornaments."

Monkey-eating eagle

This huge, rare bird once lived in the canopy of the Indonesian rainforests. But now there are probably less than 50 pairs left. They have been killed and stuffed as trophies.

Tiger, tiger

Tigers living in the rainforest reserves in India are protected by "Operation Tiger" and their numbers are slowly increasing. But outside the reserves tigers are still hunted.

Feather frenzy!

The feathers of the beautiful forest birds are used for ceremonial headdresses by forest people like the Kayapo tribe of the Amazon (left). But the birds are threatened more by outsiders who catch them, bundle them into crates, and sell them abroad as pets. Feathers were also once fashionable for decorating European ladies' hats.

TALKING POINT

Throughout the history of the world, countless animals and plants have died out. But rainforest animals and plants are becoming extinct more quickly than ever before.

Q: How quickly do you think rainforest animals are disappearing and why are they disappearing so fast?

A: No one really knows but scientists guess at least one kind, or species, of animal or plant is lost every day. They are dying out so fast today because we are destroying their forest homes and food supplies.

Lost Chances

Doctors already use many medicines that came originally from the rainforest, and there are likely to be many more still to be found. But if the forests are destroyed and the knowledge of the forest people is lost, we may never know what they are.

◀ Scientists

Many scientists are at work in the rainforests. Some study the animals, counting them, watching their behavior, and discovering new kinds. Others study the plants, looking for new types that may provide us with new medicines or better food. But some (left) have the job of studying the effects of the destruction when the chances of finding interesting new species are gone.

Native herbalists ▶

Native healers, sometimes called medicine men, witch doctors, or shamans, know which plants have healing properties — they have been using them for thousands of years. This knowledge, passed on by word of mouth from generation to generation, is in danger of being lost as native populations decline. Without this knowledge, it will take scientists much longer to test all the plants — and they may not have much longer!

◀ Sausage tree

A cream made from the two-foot-(60cm-) long, sausage-shaped fruits of this tropical African tree is successful as a treatment for skin complaints such as eczema and psoriasis.

Helpful rainforest

Many plants make medicine-like chemicals, not for our benefit, but to keep nibbling animals away. Rainforest plants are no exception, and over 1,000 plants from South America alone have already been tested as potentially helpful medicines. Some of them that are already in use include treatments for stomach cancer and leukemia, breathing difficulties and coughs, blood pressure and heart problems, and dysentery and malaria.

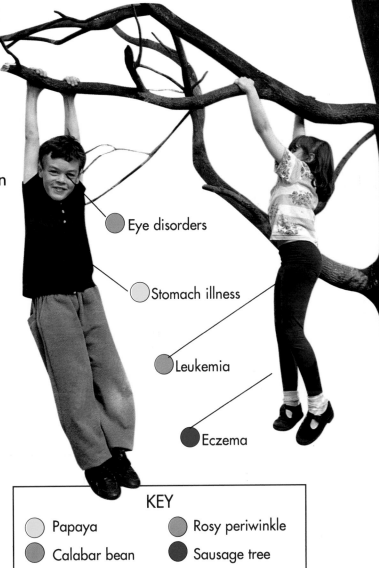

Eye disorders

Stomach illness

Leukemia

Eczema

KEY

- Papaya
- Calabar bean
- Rosy periwinkle
- Sausage tree

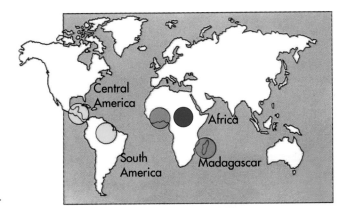

Central America

Africa

South America

Madagascar

TALKING POINT

Thousands of plants, many from tropical forests, are used for traditional medicines around the world.

Q: Can they be grown on farms?

A: No. Most rainforest plants are very picky about where they grow. If the rainforests are destroyed, the possible cures for many of our diseases may be lost forever.

CHAPTER FIVE
Solutions

Stopping the Destruction

We must find a way of saving the rainforests before time runs out. The short-sighted wide-scale destruction must be replaced by careful harvesting of renewable products, so that people can benefit, and the plants and animals can recover.

Eco-tourism

In some parts of the world, the animals and plants in tropical forests are protected in reserves. One way to help pay for the management of these reserves is by eco-tourism, where visitors pay to go on jungle safaris. They experience for themselves the humid, dank atmosphere, smell the musty smells, hear the weird cries of the canopy creatures, and see the beautiful colors of the flowers, birds, and butterflies.

Elephant power

Asian elephants are quite at home in the jungle. They can carefully lift, push, and haul logs, in any kind of terrain. They are still used in the jungles of Myanmar to bring in much of the valuable teak harvest. Unlike the wheels of a truck, elephants need no roads and do no lasting damage to forest plants.

Sting!

Although many international celebrities have tried to alert the world to the plight of the rainforests, one of the most famous is the rock star Sting (below). He has visited the Amazon jungle many times and befriended the forest people. He has done much to publicize the need to restore the forests to the native people and to conserve (protect) the plants and animals.

One elephant can haul a log weighing more than 4 tons — two together can handle even greater weights.

Q: What advantages do they have over logging machines? Think about food verses fuel, and damage done.

A: Trained elephants know their job and need little supervision. They do not damage surrounding plants or frighten forest animals. They feed on renewable plant food and don't use up gas or pollute the atmosphere. They also help to fertilize the forest soil with their droppings.

Reafforestation

The destruction of the forests is called deforestation. The replacement of the forests is called reafforestation. In some patches of cleared forest, local people are planting and caring for seedling jungle trees (right). Eventually, they will be able to harvest the fruits of these trees.

Look Back and Find

How much do you know about the rainforests? Here are some questions, and you can look back to find out the answers. There are also some extra facts that will help you to become even more of an expert.

Around the world

What is the temperature in tropical rainforests? What are the different types of rainforest? Some scientists think that the montane forests are slowly losing their cloud cover because the world is getting warmer. Some of the animals are moving farther up the mountains to find the damp conditions that they like.

Rainforest trees

What are the different layers in a rainforest called? What sort of supports help to hold the trees up? How do the plant leaves cope with the heavy rain? Many understory plants have no roots in the ground. They are called air plants. Their roots run along the tree branches and get their water from the rain that drenches them.

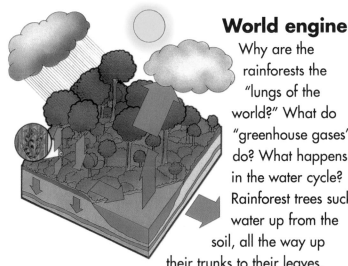

World engine

Why are the rainforests the "lungs of the world?" What do "greenhouse gases" do? What happens in the water cycle? Rainforest trees suck water up from the soil, all the way up their trunks to their leaves. Some is used to make food and the rest is lost into the air through tiny holes in the leaf surface.

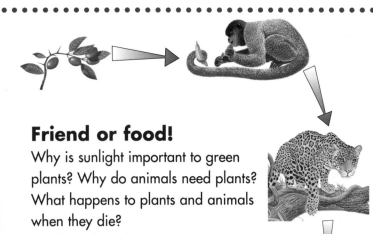

Friend or food!

Why is sunlight important to green plants? Why do animals need plants? What happens to plants and animals when they die?
The forest floor decomposers are nature's recyclers. They break all the waste down to minerals and release them into the soil, where the tree roots can take them in and use them to grow.

Animals work for plants

What do plants need animals for? Why are fruits delicious? Do plants ever eat animals?
Some rainforest flowers, like the arum lily, are very beautiful but they stink of rotting meat. This is to lure flies that are looking for dead animals to lay their eggs on. The flies bring pollen from other arum lilies.

Rainforest people

How do rainforest people get their food? What else do they get from the forest? Why are the rainforest people threatened?

Rainforest people have a very varied diet. They may range over more than 385 sq miles to gather food, but famine is unknown in a healthy forest.

Forest supermarket

What are some products from the rainforest? What sort of wood comes from rainforest trees? Where does rubber come from? Careful harvesting of natural forest products not only helps to protect the trees but also provides jobs for forest people. In Africa and Asia, the industry based on rattan, a climbing vine, employs many thousands of people.

Disappearing forests

Why are the rainforests disappearing? How long do the nutrients in the soil last after the trees have gone? Many of the countries where rainforests grow are poor and owe millions of dollars to western countries. They have to pay these debts by selling the wood.

Forest animals

Can you name some endangered forest creatures? What kinds of rare animals are sometimes kept as pets? What is being done to protect these creatures? In 1973, many countries in the world signed a treaty called CITES to ban the trade in rare plants and animals. But the trade still goes on illegally.

Herbal remedies

What are some rainforest medicines used for? Are there other medicines to be found in the forests? Why do scientists rely on forest people? The Kayapo Indians from the Amazon rainforest use over 150 types of different forest plants to treat stomach trouble alone.

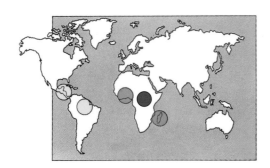

Saving the forest

How can eco-tourism help the rainforests? Why do elephants do a better job of logging than machines? Can the rainforests be restored? The governments of some rainforest countries are trying to repair the damage. In Vietnam, where the forests were destroyed by a war in the 1960s and 1970s, they aim to plant 500 million trees every year. Every school child has to plant, and care for, one tree.

You Be Environmental!

The rainforests seem a long way away. And despite all the campaigns by environmental groups and scientists, the rate of destruction does not seem to be slowing down. But there is plenty that you can do to help save the rainforests. You can write to your member of congress to show your concern. You can stop buying items made at the expense of the rainforest (Friends of the Earth can give you a list of good and bad items).

You can start helping the rainforest right away by collecting and recycling paper. Be aware of how much paper you use and whether you need to use so much.

Useful addresses
Write to these organizations for more information on how you can get involved.

Wildlife Conservation International
The New York Zoological Society
Bronx Zoo
Bronx, NY 10460

Friends of the Earth
530 7th Street SE
Washington, DC 20003

Greenpeace
1436 U Street NW
Washington, DC 20009

Exotic plants and pets
Don't buy exotic plants and animals, such as orchids and parrots, if they were captured from the wild. Many of these creatures are already rare in the wild. When caught, they are kept in terrible conditions until sold, so that many of them die. This kind of cruelty doesn't have to go on.

GLOSSARY

Bacteria
Very tiny living things, sometimes called germs, that are too small to see with the naked eye.

Canopy
The top main layer of the rainforest where the tree branches spread out.

Carbon dioxide
One of the gases that makes up the air; it is needed by plants so they can make food; it is also a main greenhouse gas.

Carnivores
Animals that eat only other animals.

Condense
To turn from a gas or vapor to a liquid, like steam (water vapor) turns to water.

Conservation
Protecting plants and animals from extinction.

Decomposers
Animals, fungi, and bacteria that feed on dead plants and animals.

Ecosystem
All the plants and animals that live together in one place and depend upon each other for food, shelter, or reproduction.

Endangered species
Very rare animals and plants that may die out.

Energy
The power that makes things happen. Plants and animals get it from their food and use it to grow and reproduce.

Evaporate
When a liquid turns to a gas or vapor. For example, when wet laundry dries, the water turns into water vapor in the air.

Extinction
When all the plants or animals of one specific kind have died.

Greenhouse gases
Certain gases in the air that act like the glass in a greenhouse — they let the sunlight in but do not let all the heat out, so the earth gets hotter and hotter.

Herbivores
Animals that eat only plants.

Pollination
Moving pollen from one flower to another so that the seeds inside the flowers can develop.

Pollution
All the poisons and garbage that are filling the air and the water and covering the land.

Recycling
Using things again and again before throwing them away, so that less raw materials from the earth are used up.

Reforestation
Planting young trees in an area where forest destruction, or deforestation, has taken place.

Understory
The layer in the rainforest beneath the canopy, where most of the smaller plants grow.

INDEX

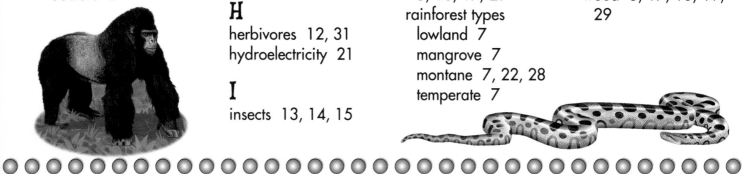

Picture Credits

Abbreviations: t-top, m-middle, b-bottom, r-right, l-left, c-center.

Cover & Pages 6, 7ml, 10, 11, 13, 18, 21 all, 23, 24t & 27 both - Frank Spooner Pictures. 4, 5, 17, 19ml & mc & 20 - Eye Ubiquitous. 7t, mr & b, 19mr & 26 - Spectrum Colour Library. 24t & 25t - Oxford Scientific Films. 25m - Roger Vlitos.